The Lighter Side of

Dark Chocolate

Take it to Heart

The Lighter Side of Dark Chocolate

Take it to Heart

by

George Rapitis, MS. Nutritionist

AuthorHouse™
1663 Liberty Drive
Bloomington, IN 47403
www.authorhouse.com
Phone: 833-262-8899

This book is printed on acid-free paper.

ISBN: 978-1-4343-0231-1 (sc)

Print information available on the last page.

Published by AuthorHouse 02/25/2021

authorHOUSE®

Introduction

The health benefits of chocolate have always had a long history dating back thousands of years. Legend has it that Montezuma, the great Aztec emperor who was the ruler of a extraordinary civilization in central Mexico in the 1st millennium AD, drank 50 golden chalices daily filled with chocolate as dense as molasses. Even then, chocolate was a luxury held with great regard. Much later in history, Christopher Columbus was credited with bringing cacoa beans to Spain following his third journey to the New World in 1502-1504.

In more recent times, during World War II, the U.S. government recognized chocolate's role in the nourishment and morale of the Allied Armed Forces, that it made special room for the shipping and importation of chocolate bars to troops. Many soldiers appreciated the quick boost of energy and nourishment received when eating them, until more food supplies were made available. Taking example from the military, U.S. astronauts have taken chocolate bars with them into space as part of their diet and nourishment.

Chocolate has also had a spiritual impact on the history of civilization. Theobroma, the tropical tree that chocolate is made from, is the Greek word for "food of the gods." Interestingly, Aztec Indians believed chocolate contained special powers which were discovered during their time period. The Aztec Indian legend held that cacao seeds had been brought from Paradise and that wisdom and power came from eating the fruit of the cocoa tree. Because of a spelling error, the cacao beans became known as the cocoa beans. When the Spanish general, Hernando

Cortes, journeyed to Mexico in 1519, the Aztecs believed he was the reincarnation of one of their lost gods. They showed him honor by serving him an unusual drink, presented in a chalice of pure gold. The Aztecs called this unusual drink "chocolatl". When Cortes returned to Spain, he took the cocoa bean with him and there it was mixed with sugar and vanilla. Ever since that time, chocolate became a food that eventually made its way around to countries all over the world.

One of the countries that chocolate made its way too was Switzerland. Some of the finest chocolate is made in Switzerland, where the consumption of milk chocolate far exceeds that of plain chocolate. In the United States of America, the production of chocolate proceeded at a faster pace than anywhere else in the world. It was during pre-revolutionary New England — 1765, that the first chocolate factory was established in America. In 1875, Henri Nestlé collaborated with a neighboring manufacturer in Vevey, Switzerland to invent his formula for milk chocolate. It was there that inventor Daniel Peter added Nestlé condensed milk to his chocolate to create Nestlé milk chocolate.

In the 1900s, Milton S. Hershey worked zealously at preparing a recipe that would compete with the Swiss until he finally came out with a formula which mixed the right combination of sugar and cocoa. This formula was so amazingly popular with the public that he began to mass produce and distribute chocolate candy very successfully.

In 1903, Hershey's company began producing milk chocolate in bars, wafers and other shapes. The demand for the company's chocolate became so great that Hershey began to distribute his product in large quantities. The result was that Hershey was able to lower the per unit cost and making milk chocolate, once an item more easily affordable to the wealthy, finally a food that was affordable to people of all income levels. One early advertising slogan described this new product as "a palatable confection and a most nourishing food". As a result of Hershey's and other companies, chocolate has made history by becoming America's favorite flavor. A recent survey revealed that 52 percent of U.S. adults said they like chocolate best.

Chocolate making has undergone an interesting transformation since the historical days of the Aztec Indians. For example, because of recent studies about the correlation of the antioxidants in dark chocolate and heart health, Hershey's has created a new line of dark chocolate bars. Consumers can now purchase "Extra Dark" chocolate bars that contain antioxidant foods such as almonds, cranberries and blueberries.

In addition, the recent studies at leading universities such as Yale and Harvard have now shown that regular consumers of dark chocolate appear to be reaping the heart healthy benefits. "If chocolate has a high cocoa content, it is the most concentrated source of natural flavanol antioxidants in our diet," claims Dr. David Katz, director of the Yale University Prevention and Research Center. "It is even better than green tea"

Chapter 1

Ingredients and Preparation of Cocoa

Chocolate is prepared using beans harvested from the cocoa tree an evergreen typically grown within 20 degrees of the equator. They are removed from their pod, fermented, dried, roasted and then ground to produce a cocoa dry mass or cocoa liquor. The cocoa dry mass is then pressed to yield cocoa butter and cocoa cake that is then ground.

From Cocoa Bean to Cocoa Mass

Cocoa solids and cocoa liquor, are often terms used interchangeably, however they are quite different. When the meat or "nib" of the cocoa bean is ground into a smooth liquid, it is called chocolate liquor. However, if the chocolate maker removes all the fat (or cocoa butter, which comprises 53 percent of the bean) from the chocolate liquor, cocoa solid mass such as cocoa powder is what remains. This powder is used in various chocolate drinks such as hot cocoa as well as the basis for cocoa butter.

Cocoa Butter Explained

Cocoa butter is the main ingredient in many chocolate bars. It is the ivory colored natural fat of the cocoa bean extracted during the manufacturing process of producing chocolate and cocoa powder. Cocoa butter has a very subtle mellow flavor that gives chocolate its creamy and smooth texture that allows the chocolate to melt in the mouth of the consumer. Cocoa butter helps to provide a delicious food that gives temporary nourishment.

Chapter 2

Dark Chocolate 101

In the United States, the Food and Drug Administration (FDA) has established standards of identity for many chocolate and cocoa products. These standards designate the percentage of key ingredients that must be present. In general, chocolate manufacturers make three different types of chocolate: milk chocolate, dark chocolate, and white chocolate.

Milk Chocolate Explained

In order for milk chocolate to be classified as milk chocolate, it must contain at least 10 percent chocolate liquor, 20 percent milk solids, and 3.7 percent milk fats ("Types of Chocolate", n.d.). It is generally mixed with vanilla, butter, cocoa, sugar and lecithin. Milk chocolate is most often used in chocolate bars but it can also be found in cakes, pies and in many desserts. Its sweet flavor makes it a popular choice whereas dark chocolate is more of an acquired taste.

Dark Chocolate Explained

Unlike milk chocolate, dark chocolate contains a higher amount of chocolate liquor which causes it to produce a more bitter taste, compared to milk chocolate which is smooth and sweet. This is why dark chocolate is also known as "bittersweet" or "semisweet" chocolate.

Because each must contain at least 35 percent chocolate liquor, bittersweet chocolate, semi-sweet chocolate, and dark chocolate are different names for the same thing. In addition, dark chocolate contains much more cocoa than other forms of chocolate.

White Chocolate Explained

White chocolate is a type of chocolate that is based on cocoa butter without the cocoa solids which actually does not qualify as a chocolate. While the ingredients in white chocolate do contain milk solids, sugar, lecithin, and flavorings such as vanilla it contains no chocolate liquor. Because it contains cocoa butter, it remains solid at room temperature just like regular chocolate however, white chocolate has a different taste. It also does not contain caffeine while milk chocolate and dark chocolate do contain a small amount.

---

* Types of Chocolate. (n.d.). Retrieved February 5, 2007, from http://www.hersheys.com/nutrition/chocolate.asp

Chapter 3
Yes, Believe It,
Chocolate Can Be Good For You!

The beneficial plant compounds in chocolate are called flavonoids, which contribute to the dark pigment in chocolate. Dark chocolate contains a high percentage (equal to 70 percent) of cocoa solids, and little or no added sugar. As a result, dark chocolate contains more health benefits. At the contrary, milk chocolate contains less flavonoids as evidenced by its lighter color.

Retaining Beneficial Compounds in Cocoa Bean

Flavonoids occur naturally in the cocoa plant as a way of protecting the plant. Their presence affects the taste of chocolate and are responsible for the astringency in the unprocessed cocoa bean ("Not all chocolate", n.d.). It is crucial that the plant flavonoids in dark chocolate stay intact while processing, otherwise important nutrients may be harmed, thus decreasing the nutritional value of the dark chocolate.

Proprietary Processes that Prevent Loss of Flavonoids

While flavonoids are naturally found in the cocoa plant, it is the process by which the cocoa is handled that determines the amount of flavonoids in the finished product. One of the chocolate manufacturers that use methods which retain more flavonoids, is Mars Incorporated (Inc.). In Mars Inc. chocolate, products, the levels of raw cocoa are retained through proprietary processes that help prevdestruction of the cocoa flavonoids during processing. Products made with these processes carry the trademark Cocoapro. Manufacturing processes such as fermentation and roasting can affect the levels of flavonoids that are in the final chocolate product ("Nutrients in Chocolate", n.d.). When cocoa is processed into Cocoapro chocolate products, it goes through several steps that help to develop the flavor of chocolate and determine the amount of flavonoids retained in the finished chocolate product.

---

*Not All Chocolate Is Created Equal. (n.d.). Retrieved February 9, 2007, from http://www.cocoapro.com/process/articles/not_equal.jsp

*Nutrients In Chocolate Explained. (n.d.). Retrieved February 9, 2007, from http://www.cocoapro.com/cnhy/choc_healthy/cyh308.jsp

Chapter 4

Nutrients In Dark Chocolate

Make "Brown" Beautiful!

New studies show that beneficial nutrients can be found in dark chocolate. This has encouraged nutrition professionals to educate people on how dark chocolate can be included in a healthy eating plan. In fact, registered dietitian Althea Zanecosky, American Dietetic Association spokesperson, claims that "Cocoa contains the same nutrients found in other plant foods, including minerals and specific antioxidants that help ward off diseases such as heart disease." In addition, she suggests, "oleic acid, a monounsaturated fat also found in olive oil, makes up one-third of the fat in chocolate and has been shown to be beneficial for heart health." as cited in Mcmannon, (2003). Since cocoa in dark chocolate is so rich in flavonoids, several chocolate companies have begun manufacturing candy bars that contain as much as 80 percent cocoa.

Flavonoids in Dark Chocolate

Flavonoids are the biggest class of antioxidants which have been closely studied. In fact, nature provides thousands of different antioxidants in various amounts in fruits, vegetables, whole grains, nuts, and legumes. When the human body needs to defend itself from toxins that are often found in today's environment, antioxidants are crucial to preserving health.

In addition, flavonoids keep cholesterol from gathering in blood vessels, reducing the risk of blood clots, and slowing down the immune responses that lead to clogged arteries. They contain several subgroups such as polyphenols, catechins, and epicatchins.

---

*Mcmannon, B. (2003). For the love of chocolate: Chocolate is good for the heart. *Journal of the American Dietetic Association.* Retrieved February 14, 2007, from http://www.eatright.org/cps/rde/xchg/ada/hs.xsl/media_3074_ENU_HTML.htm

Polyphenols

One of the nutrients in dark chocolate is called a polyphenol. Polyphenols are apart of a large family of natural compounds found in a wide variety of plant foods. Furthermore, polyphenols are a smaller class of antioxidants, which scientists often refer to as "phenols." They are helpful in assisting the human body protect itself from free radicals that cause oxidation. Free radicals are unstable, highly reactive forms of oxygen that can attack the cells of the human body. They are natural by-products of metabolism and are also formed in the body as a result of smoking, air pollution and exposure to sunlight. However, antioxidants such as polyphenols, help protect the body against the damage from these free radicals. In addition, phenols are potent antioxidants that prevent LDL, the "bad" cholesterol, in the body from building plaque in the arteries. In fact, feeding studies in humans showed that LDL cholesterol in the blood taken two hours past consumption of chocolate was less likely to oxidize as cited in Blumberg, (2006).

Catechins

Another type of polyphenol in dark chocolate is called a catechin. It is known as a simple flavonoid. A catechin aids in resistance against degenerative diseases such as heart disease. A catechin can also be found in fruits and vegetables, but the body needs to capture as many different types of catechins as possible. Dark chocolate can help the body absorb the various kinds of catechins, due to its high concentration of cocoa.

Epicatechins

A more complex flavonoid found in dark chocolate is called an epicatechin. According to Ofstein, "Dark chocolate contains epicatechin, which is a compound of plant flavonoids. These flavonoids can help keep cholesterol from gathering in blood vessels and reduce the risk of blood clots" as cited in McKee, (2007). Epicatechin, is also a nutrient that may be found in certain fruit and vegetables, green teas, red wine and purple grape juice. However, it is especially abundant in certain cocoas.

Moreover, epicatechins are directly associated with improved circulation and help to promote the cardiovascular health of the arteries of the heart. It is a particularly active member of a group of compounds that can help fight arteriosclerosis. In orderto receive the benefits of flavonoids such as epicatechin, researchers suggest consuming the most nutritious dark chocolate.

For example, this means if a dark chocolate is combined with ice creams, chocolate flavored gums, and caramel it is most likely full of empty calories that have little health benefit.

Research and Data Analysis

One Italian study by Christina Lippi, demonstrated how chocolate polyphenols affected platelet activation proteins in a positive manner. When platelets that were exposed to chocolate polyphenols were stimulated with epinephrine (known to cause platelet aggregation) aggregation actually decreased, thus reducing the risk of blood clot formation as cited in Lippi, (2005). The results emphasize that the polyphenolic structure of flavonoids has two positive effects on the cardiovascular system.

---

* Blumberg, J. B. (2005). Microplate-based Oxygen Radical Absorbance Capacity (ORAC) assay of hydrophilic and lipophilic compartments in plasma. *Nutrition Science. 9,* 48-54.

*McKee, S. (2007). The dark side of chocolate: Healthy or hype? Retrieved February 14, 2007, from http://www.ediets.com/news/article.cfm/cmi_2330335/cid_1/code_30171

*Lippi, C. (2005). Short-term administration of dark chocolate is followed by a significant increase in insulin sensitivity and a decrease in blood pressure in healthy persons. *American Journal of Clinical Nutrition, 8,* 611-4.

First, antioxidants help to prevent arterial damage caused by free radicals which damage the arterial walls by blocking the artery wall lining. A certain amount of oxidation in the body is necessary in order to fight infections or do repair work within cells.

However, when a shift in oxidation exceeds normal levels this leads to a dangerous amount of oxidation as cited in Sahelian, (n.d.). Without adequate antioxidant support, the body undergoes what is called "oxidative stress". The body normally produces powerful natural antioxidants—such as superoxide dismutase, glutathione, and catalase—to help fight these oxidants called free radicals.

According to Blumberg (2006), "Free radicals trigger a damaging chain reaction, and that is the crux of the problem." He also believes that, "Free radicals are dangerous because they do not just damage one molecule, but can set off a whole chain reaction. In addition, when a free radical oxidizes a fatty acid, it changes that fatty acid into a free radical, which then damages another fatty acid. It is a very rapid chain reaction" (p.1366). These external attacks can overwhelm the natural free-radical defense system of the body. In time, and with repeated free radical attacks that the body cannot stop, that damage can lead to a multitude of chronic diseases, including heart disease. However, antioxidants such as flavonoids, which are also consumed through a healthy diet that includes foods such as dark chocolate, appear to reverse this process.

Second, flavonoids inhibit platelet aggregation, because they prevent blood cells from clotting which could cause a heart attack or stroke. Dark chocolate is so high in important heart healthy nutrients, that it contains more flavonoids than any other antioxidant rich food -- including green tea, black tea, red wine, and blueberries.

In fact, three blocks of the "Exta Dark" chocolate by Hershey's is equal to: two-thirds of a cup of blueberries, one cup of red wine, and two cups of green tea.

*Sahelian, R. (2007). Chocolate. Retrieved on February 12, 2007, from http://www.raysahelian.com/flavonoids.html

37 grams	*equals*	2/3 cup	*equals*	1 cup	*equals*	2 cups
3 squares		blueberries		red wine		green tea

Figure 3. Depicted in figure 3 is the flavonoid comparison of "Extra Dark" chocolate with other antioxidant containing foods Source: The Hershey's Company. Retrieved April 24, 2007, at http://www.hersheys.com/nutrition/antioxidants.asp

In addition, a 40gram dark chocolate bar contains between 205-300mg of polyphenols, which compares favorbly to a five ounce glass of red wine that contains 210mg of polyphenols and has been associated with reducing the risk of developing heart disease. Further evidence of dark chocolate's rich antioxidant content is its measure of Oxygen Radical Absorbance Capacity (ORAC), which is a measure of antioxidant power. Because foods may contain different types of antioxidants, ORAC, compares various antioxidant rich foods. Data from the U.S. Department of Agriculture indicates that dark chocolate is at the very top of the list for ORAC on a per serving basis. It contains 9080 units per serving ("Antioxidants", n.d.).

*Source: The Hershey's Company. Retrieved April 24, 2007 at http://www.hersheys.com/nutrition/antioxidants.asp

Chapter 5
Dark Chocolate and Your Heart — A Happy Marriage

Statistics of Cardiovascular Disease and Prevention

More then 910,000 Americans die of cardiovascular disease every year, and some 70 million Americans are living with it, according to the U.S. Centers for Disease Control and Prevention (Green, 2007). Heart attacks, strokes, often the leading causes of death are among the nations leading causes of death. Eating the right kinds of foods, exercise, and not smoking can make a big difference on how well the heart works. Dr. Gerald Fletcher, a spokesperson for the American Heart Association and a cardiologist at the Mayo Clinic claims, "Heart disease is not something you're born with except on rare occasions. It's an acquired disease, something that can be prevented" (Green, 2007, p.4).

Blood Pressure and Dark Chocolate

High blood pressure is a very serious illness that strikes nearly 1 in 3 American adults (AHA, n.d.). High blood pressure is a blood pressure reading of 140/90 mmHg or higher. Both numbers are extremely important. Once high blood pressure develops, a person can expect to have it for the rest of his life. High blood pressure has various treatments such as medications called diuretics but no cure. High blood pressure is called the silent killer because it usually has no symptoms.

---

*Green, A. (2007, February 4). Prescription for A Healthy Heart. *American Profile.* pp. 3-10.

*American Heart Association. (2007). Factors that contribute to high blood pressure. Retrieved February 7, 2007, from http://www.americanheart.org/ presenter.jtml?identifier=4650

Some people may not find out they have it until they have trouble with their heart, brain, or kidneys. When high blood pressure is not found and treated, it can cause the heart to grow larger, which may lead to heart failure. It can also lead to small bulges that may form in blood vessels. Very common locations where these small bulges can occur are in the main artery from in the heart (aorta). High blood pressure can also cause kidney failure due to the narrowing of the blood vessels in that area. Arteries throughout the body harden faster, especially those in the heart and brain.

Research Supporting Dark Chocolate Helping Lower High Blood Pressure

Current research supports that eating more dark chocolate can help lower blood pressure. Plant phenols -- cocoa phenols, to be exact, found in dark chocolate, appear to have a blood pressure decreasing effect. According to Taubert, Berkels, Roesen, & Klaus, (2003), at the University of Cologne, Germany, "Dark chocolate not white chocolate lowers high blood pressure" (p. 1029).

Taubert et al., signed up six men and seven women aged 55-64 for the study. All subjects had just been diagnosed with mild high blood pressure -- on average, systolic blood pressure (the top number) of 153 and diastolic blood pressure (the bottom number) of 84. Every day for two weeks, they ate a 100-gram candy bar and were asked to balance its 480 calories by not eating other foods similar in nutrients and calories. Half the patients received dark chocolate and half received white chocolate. Those who ate dark chocolate had a significant drop in blood pressure (by an average of five points for systolic and an average of two points for diastolic blood pressure). Those who ate white chocolate did not as cited in Taubert et al., (2003). The results from this study appear to show the beneficial effects of dark chocolate on lowering high blood pressure compared to white chocolate, which does not contain antioxidant flavonoids.

---

*Taubert, D., Berkels, R., Roesen, R. & Klaus, W. (2003). Chocolate and blood pressure in elderly individuals with isolated systolic hypertension. *Journal of the American Medical Association, 290,* 1029-103.

Taubert et al., signed up six men and seven women aged 55-64 for the study. All subjects had just been diagnosed with mild high blood pressure -- on average, systolic blood pressure (the top number) of 153 and diastolic blood pressure (the bottom number) of 84. Every day for two weeks, they ate a 100-gram candy bar and were asked to balance its 480 calories by not eating other foods similar in nutrients and calories. Half the patients received dark chocolate and half received white chocolate. Those who ate dark chocolate had a significant drop in blood pressure (by an average of five points for systolic and an average of two points for diastolic blood pressure). Those who ate white chocolate did not as cited in Taubert et al., (2003). The results from this study appear to show the beneficial effects of dark chocolate on lowering high blood pressure compared to white chocolate, which does not contain antioxidant flavonoids.

Research Correlating Aortic Elasticity with Dark Chocolate

Researchers have found that dietary compounds in dark chocolate, especially have been shown to have pronounced positive effects on endothelial function as cited in Vita, (2005).

In order to prevent damage to arteries, current research suggests that dark chocolate can help prevent the oxidation of LDL "bad" cholesterol and its ensuing damage to coronary arteries ("Chocolate as a health", 2005). In fact, two studies testing dark chocolate or cocoa found significant improvement in overall function of the endothelium in healthy volunteers as cited in DeNoon, (2003). These studies investigated the positive effects of dark chocolate in participants with high blood pressure and found 100g of dark chocolate fed for 15 days produced significant improvements in endothelial function as well as other health factors related to insulin resistance and blood pressure as cited in Grassi, (2005). Perhaps the most interesting and meaningful observation of endothelial function studies is the underlying physiological mechanism, which is influenced by cocoa flavonols and nitric oxide.

Nitric oxide and Dark Chocolate Connection

Nitric oxide is produced in the vascular endothelium and acts as a signaling molecule for arteries to properly dilate when necessary. Niaomi Fisher, who discovered this effect, was awarded the 1998 Nobel Prize for Medicine. It is the basic mechanistic premise for pharmaceuticals designed for vascular disorders.

---

*Vita, J. A. (2005). Polyphenols and cardiovascular disease: effects on endothelial and platelet function. *American Journal of Clinical Nutrition, 81*, 292S-7S.

Longest Clinical Study of Aortic Elasticity and Dark Chocolate

In addition, there is solid research that regular consumers of dark chocolate may find beneficial. According to Mary Engler, of the University of California, San Francisco, "eating a small, 1.6-ounce bar of dark chocolate daily can be beneficial to the heart" as cited in Denoon, (2003). In her study, Engler divided 21 healthy adults into two groups. One group got a Dove Dark Chocolate bar every day for two weeks. Like other dark chocolate bars with high-cocoa content, it is highly loaded with the flavonoid epicatechin. The second group that didn't get Dove bars was not totally left out. They, too, received dark chocolate bars. However, their chocolate had the flavonoids taken out. All subjects underwent high tech evaluation of how well the blood vessels dilate and relax, an indictor of healthy blood vessel function. Blood vessel stiffness indicates diseased vessels and possible atherosclerosis.

Those who received the full-flavonoid chocolate did significantly better as cited in Denoon, (2003). Blood tests showed that high levels of epicatechin were coursing through their arteries as cited in Denoon, (2003). According to Engler, "This is the longest clinical trial to date to show improvement in blood vessel function from consuming flavonoid-rich dark chocolate daily over an extended period of time." Engler goes on to claim, "It is likely that the elevated blood levels of epicatechin triggered the release of active substances that increase blood flow in the artery. Better blood flow is good for your heart" as cited in Denoon, (2003).

In another additional test by Engler, such as one randomized, double-blind, placebo-controlled study, eleven people received 46 grams (1.6 ounces) of dark, flavonoid-rich chocolate every day for two weeks, while ten others received dark chocolate with low-flavonoid content. At the end of the two-week trial, Engler recorded the ability of the principal artery in the arm, the brachial artery, to expand. The brachial artery's dilation measurements correlate well with those of the coronary arteries that supply the heart. Afterward, the team measured the artery's "flow-mediated dilation" using ultrasound to obtain the brachial artery's diameter immediately after deflating a blood pressure cuff that had been inflated for five minutes on study participants' forearms as cited in DeNoon, (2003).

*Denoon, D. (2003, August 27). Dark chocolate has health benefits not seen in other varieties. Retrieved February 7, 2007, from http://www.webmd.com/ content/article/73/91921

*Grassi, D. (2005b). Short-term administration of dark chocolate is followed by a significant increase in insulin sensitivity and a decrease in blood pressure in healthy persons. *American Journal of Clinical Nutrition, 81,* 611-4.

Chapter 6
Overview of Good Blood Flow
and Dark Chocolate

Good blood flow is essential to how the circulatory system functions. The basic action of the blood moving from cell to cell is of great importance to the health and longevity of a healthy individual. In specific, circulatory disorders are quite common in the middle-aged and especially in the elderly. As a result of circulatory disorders, a heart attack very often occurs because the blood flow to the heart is blocked, most commonly by a blood clot blocking a coronary artery. Almost all types of heart disease have one thing in common: there is a certain type of obstruction of blood flow in the circulatory system. When the blood flow in the body is not flowing properly it can affect on the performance of the heart in a negative manner. Poor blood flow could be compared to extreme traffic buildup on a major expressway when cars are moving at a slow rate. There are several reasons for poor blood flow in the circulatory system.

Reasons for Insufficient Blood Flow

One of the reasons the blood flow in the heart may be poor, is the presence of plaque formation which can restrict or even slow down blood flow. Poor blood flow can affect and damage the blood vessel wall and and/or promotes blood clot formation. Another reason is that plaque can cause calcification of blood vessels. This is caused by the buildup of calcium deposits that makes blood vessel walls rigid and fragile, otherwise known as "narrowing of the arteries." In the inner lining of the endothelium, platelets can aggregate (clump) and adhere to the site of an injury (caused by LDL cholesterol or other factors in blood) and subsequently contribute the development of plaques. This is one of the key reasons that blood clots usually form in coronary arteries that have already been narrowed by plaque formation associated with coronary artery disease (CAD).

Consequences s of Insufficient Blood Flow to the Heart

People with coronary artery disease may also experience other acute coronary syndromes that may precede or coincide with a heart attack including:

1   various types of angina (chest pain due to insufficient blood flow to heart muscle).

2   sudden death (abrupt death due to a serious disturbance in the heart's rhythm).

When the body is resting or performing routine activities, the heart muscle may be receiving just enough blood. But it may not be enough to supply the heart muscle during periods of increased oxygen demand, such as during physical exercise or emotional stress. A person whose blood vessels have been narrowed by 70 percent or more may experience angina (AHA, n.d.). Symptoms include tightness, pressure, or burning sensation in the chest, which may spread to the arms, left shoulder, neck, or jaw. Other reasons for poor blood flow include bleeding or hemorrhage, and embolize which is when a tiny piece of plaque breaks off and travels to distant locations through the body's blood vessels.

Research on the Correlation of Cocoa and Platelet Activity

A decrease in platelet activity is favorable to overall cardiovascular health. Currently, several clinical trials have investigated the effects of cocoa and platelet activity. After drinking cocoa high in polyphenols, a reduction platelet activation was found, as was a decreased formation of platelet "microparticles"—which are linked to the development of blood clots. The researchers concluded that eating cocoa had an "aspirin effect" on blood-clotting mechanisms as cited in Rein, (2000).

In addition, cocoa in dark chocolate may be beneficial to blood flow because it helps relax and dilate blood vessels, so blood flows more easily. Dr. Vlachopoulos, at the University of Athens, Greece, showed this health benefit. In his study, Vlachopoulos asked 17 healthy volunteers to eat a candy bar made by the Nestle's company and then used ultrasound to measure the blood flow in their arteries. To rule out any possible benefit from the act of chewing, the volunteers were then asked to "simulate chewing" and had blood flow measured again.

In the study, blood flow measurements taken after the volunteers ate chocolate were much better than after the simulated chewing as cited in Vlachopoulos, (2006). Vlachopoulos believes flavonoids explain the difference. During this study, he illustrates that red wine has a high flavonoid concentration that may explain its heart benefit, but dark chocolate has even more flavonoids, suggesting that "it may provide a benefit as good as or better than red wine." He goes on to claim, "blood flow measurements taken after the volunteers ate chocolate were much better than after the simulated chewing" (p.205). As a result of the study, dark chocolate significantly improved the smoothness of arterial flow, an effect which lasted for eight hours. Antioxidant levels rose sharply in the volunteers who ate dark chocolate, because of the high levels of antioxidant flavonoids. Chocolate also appeared to slow clotting and on average, platelets in the chocoholics took 130 seconds to stick together, while in the control group about 123 seconds. Furthermore, a test of urine for the waste products of platelet activity found that chocolate eaters also had less activity and produced fewer waste products as cited in Vlachopoulos, (2006). Vlachopoulos (2006) claims, "People who ate chocolate had markedly lower amounts of urinary excretion of this byproduct of platelet activity, which meant that the platelets are not being activated and not clumping so much in the body," Vlachopoulos went on to conclude, "The magnitude of the difference is very significant" (p. 210).

---

*Vlachopoulos, C. (2006, June 24). Effect of dark chocolate on arterial function in healthy individuals: Cocoa instead of ambrosia? *American Journal of Hypertension, 3*, 205-11.

Chapter 7
Chocolate + A Healthy Heart
= Loving Indulgence

Many consumers may question what is an acceptable amount of dark chocolate to consume in order to receive cardiovascular health benefits. There is no approved recommended amount at this time, however, the University of Michigan Integrative Medicine department believes a beneficial portion appears to be seven ounces per week, an average of one ounce per day as cited in Myklebust, (n.d.). This amount is equal to about 1 small block of the Hershey's "Extra Dark" chocolate. This serving size equals about 70 calories per block, which appears to be a sensible serving if a person does not overindulge. In addition, registered dietitian, Elizabeth Somer, a member of the American Dietetic Association, claims, "chocolate is not bad for health as long as it is consumed in small doses" as cited in Somer, (2001). Many nutrition experts agree that even though dark chocolate appears heart safe, this does not give people the opportunity to binge on chocolate.

Interactions of Milk and Alkali with Dark Chocolate Flavonoids

It appears that the consumption of milk along while eating dark chocolate decreases the body's ability to absorb the beneficial antioxidants it contains. Moreover, milk appears to bind to antioxidants, inhibiting their absorption (as cited in "Cocoa process", n.d.).

In addition, cocoa processed with alkali (also called "Dutch" cocoa) increases the pH of the product and decreases the flavonoid levels. Alkali is often added to chocolates, cocoa powders, and cocoa drinks mixes for flavor. Checking food labels of chocolate products is very useful in order to determine whether the chocolate has been processed with alkali.

---

*Myklebust, M. (2007). Facts about dark chocolate. Article retrieved on February 14, 2007, from http://www.med.umich.edu/umim/clinical/pyramid/chocolate.htm

* Somer, E. (2007). For Love and Chocolate. Article retrieved from http://www.elizabethsomer.com/thoughts_detail.php?id=05

Recipes For the Heart

Tuxedo Dipped Strawberries

Ingredients
10 Strawberries washed with stem
1 pound   Dark chocolate melted
1 pound   White chocolate melted

Method

1. Place clean strawberries in cold water and pat dry with paper towels.

2. Melt in two glass microwave safe bowls, both chocolates using a microwave and by stirring it until the chocolate is warm, but not hot.

3. Line a small cookie pan with parchment paper and dip the strawberry in the white chocolate first by gently gripping the stem (coat 3/4's up). Place the strawberry on the paper and chill in the refrigerator for 5 minutes.

4. Next dip the strawberry in the dark chocolate (using the same technique) and coat both sides creating a V pattern. Looking at the strawberry the dark chocolate should touch at bottom and the remaining white chocolate should look like a tuxedo shirt without studs. Put the berry back on the parchment and refrigerate for another 5 minutes.

5. Create the studs and the tie use a paper pastry bag (or a very small artist paint brush) and fill it with a small amount of the dark chocolate and pipe 3 to 4 dots (studs) and small bow tie.

6. Remove the strawberries with flat wide knife and present on a mirror, marble piece or silver tray with a small amount of flowers.

Chocolate Crepes

Ingredients
2 eggs
1/2 cup milk
1/2 cup water
3/4 cup all-purpose flour
6 teaspoons white sugar
1/3 tablespoon butter or
margarine
1 fluid ounce Vanilla extract
1 (3.9 ounce) package instant chocolate pudding

Method
1. Crepe batter: in a large bowl, mix together eggs, milk, water, flour, sugar, 1 teaspoon butter, and vanilla extract.
2. Filling: beat pudding mix, instant coffee and whipping cream together with an electric mixer until the mixture is thick.
3. Sauce: in a small saucepan, melt the chocolate, butter, evaporated milk, and confectioners' sugar together until the mixture is a little thick.
4. Crepes: heat a small skillet (or crepe pan) to a high temperature. Place a small amount of batter into the skillet and swirl it around until the batter covers the bottom of the pan. When the crepe is slightly browned flip the crepe over and let the other side brown for a few seconds. Stack the crepes on top of each other to let tem cool before filling.
5. Spoon the filling into the center of each crepe and roll the crepe up around it. Spoon the sauce over the crepes and serve.

Low Fat Chocolate Muffins

Ingredients
 1-1/2 cups all-purpose flour
 3/4 cup granulated sugar
 1/4 cup dark cocoa
 2 teaspoons baking powder
 1 teaspoon baking soda
 1/2 teaspoon salt
 2/3 cup vanilla lowfat yogurt
 2/3 cup nonfat milk
 1/2 teaspoon vanilla extract
 Powdered sugar(optional)

Method
1. Heat oven to 400°F. Line muffin cups (2-1/2 inches in diameter) with paper bake cups.
2. Stir together flour, granulated sugar, cocoa, baking powder, baking soda and salt in medium bowl; stir in yogurt, milk and vanilla just until combined. Do not beat. Fill muffin cups 2/3 full with batter.
3. Bake 15 to 20 minutes or until wooden pick inserted in center comes out clean. Cool slightly in pan on wire rack. Remove from pans. Sprinkle powdered sugar over tops of muffins, if desired. Serve warm. Store, covered, at room temperature or freeze in airtight container for longer storage. 14 muffins.

Dark Chocolate Cake

Ingredients

2 cups boiling water
1 cup unsweetened cocoa powder
2 3/4 cups all-purpose flour
2 teaspoons baking soda
1/2 teaspoon baking powder
1/2 teaspoon salt
1 cup butter, softened
2 1/4 cups white sugar
2 eggs
4 egg whites
1 1/2 teaspoons vanilla extract

Method

1. Preheat oven to 350 degrees F (175 degrees C). Grease 3 - 9 inch round cake pans. In medium bowl, pour boiling water over cocoa, and whisk until smooth. Let mixture cool. Sift together flour, baking soda, baking powder and salt; set aside.
2. In a large bowl, cream butter and sugar together until light and fluffy. Beat in eggs one at time, then stir in vanilla. Add the flour mixture alternately with the cocoa mixture. Spread batter evenly between the 3 prepared pans.
3. Bake in preheated oven for 25 to 30 minutes. Allow to cool

Strawberry Chocolate Mouse Cake

Ingredients

1 cup chocolate cookie crumbs
3 tablespoons butter, melted
2 pints fresh strawberries, halved
2 cups semisweet chocolate chips
1/2 cup water
2 tablespoons light corn syrup
2 1/2 cups light whipping cream
1 tablespoon white sugar

Method

1. In a bowl, mix crumbs and butter to blend thoroughly. Press evenly onto bottom of 9 inch springform pan. Stand strawberry halves about pan, touching, side-by-side, pointed ends up, with cut sides against the side of pan; set aside.

2. Place chocolate chips in blender container. In small saucepan over medium heat, mix water and corn syrup. Bring to a boil and simmer for 1 minute. Immediately pour over chocolate chips and blend until smooth. Cool to room temperature.

3. While chocolate cools, in a large mixer bowl, beat 1 1/2 c of the cream to form stiff peaks. With a rubber spatula, fold cooled chocolate into whipped cream to blend thoroughly. Pour into prepared pan. Level top. Points of strawberries might extend about the chocolate mixture. Cover and refrigerate for 4 to 24 hours.

4. Up to 2 hours before serving, in a medium mixing bowl, beat remaining 1 c cream to form soft peaks. Add sugar. Beat to form stiff peaks. Remove side of pan. Place cake on serving plate. Pipe or dollop whipped cream onto top of cake. Arrange remaining halved strawberries on whipped cream. To serve, cut into wedges with thin knife, wiping blade between cuts.

Printed in the United States
By Bookmasters